Pay Competitiveness and Quality of Department of Defense Scientists and Engineers

Michael Gibbs

Prepared for the Office of the Secretary of Defense

National Defense Research Institute

RAND

The research described in this report was sponsored by the Office of the Secretary of Defense (OSD). The research was conducted in RAND's National Defense Research Institute, a federally funded research and development center supported by the OSD, the Joint Staff, the unified commands, and the defense agencies under Contract DASW01-95-C-0059.

Library of Congress Cataloging-in-Publication Data

Gibbs, Michael, 1962-
    Pay competitiveness and quality of Department of Defense scientists and
  engineers / Michael Gibbs.
        p. cm.
    MR-1312
    Includes bibliographical references.
    ISBN 0-8330-2981-9
    1. United States. Dept. of Defense—Officials and employees—Salaries, etc. 2.
Scientists—Salaries, etc.—United States. 3. Engineers—Salaries, etc.—United States.
4. United States—Armed Forces—Civilian employees—Salaries, etc. 5. United States.
Dept. of Defense—Officials and employees—Rating of. 6. United States—Armed
Forces—Civilian employees—Rating of. 7. Scientists—Rating of—United States. 8.
Engineers—Rating of—United States. I. Title.

    UB193 .G53 2001
    355.2'3—dc21

                                                                    2001020485

Published 2001 by RAND
1700 Main Street, P.O. Box 2138, Santa Monica, CA 90407-2138
1200 South Hayes Street, Arlington, VA 22202-5050
201 North Craig Street, Suite 102, Pittsburgh, PA 15213-1516
RAND URL: http://www.rand.org/
To order RAND documents or to obtain additional information,
contact Distribution Services: Telephone: (310) 451-7002;
Fax: (310) 451-6915; Internet: order@rand.org

This report documents one in a series of studies of civilian personnel management issues that RAND is conducting for the Department of Defense (DoD). This study examines the competitiveness of pay, and ensuing personnel outcomes, for highly skilled civilian scientists and engineers (S/Es) employed in laboratories within DoD agencies. Personnel data drawn from DoD records for the years 1982 through 1996 were used to analyze and reach findings on these issues. This report should be of interest to policymakers and researchers interested in compensation, personnel management, and federal personnel systems, and to human resources and research and development staffs in the Office of the Secretary of Defense and military services.

This research was conducted for the Deputy Assistant Secretary of Defense for Civilian Personnel Policy within the Forces and Resources Policy Center of RAND's National Defense Research Institute (NDRI). The NDRI is a federally funded research and development center sponsored by the Office of the Secretary of Defense, the Joint Staff, the unified commands, and the defense agencies.

CONTENTS

FIGURES

TABLES

This report presents an analysis of the pay competitiveness, and the quality of employees recruited and retained, for civilian scientific and engineering (S/E) positions in Department of Defense (DoD) laboratories from 1982 through 1996. Because the DoD is relying more and more heavily on high technology, the S/E group is an increasingly critical part of the DoD's workforce. In addition, dramatic changes occurred in the compensation of highly skilled workers in the private sector over the study period, but few changes occurred in the compensation system within the DoD during that time.

This study uses a longitudinal sample of personnel data on S/Es employed in the DoD labs. The data were provided to RAND by the Defense Manpower Data Center (DMDC). The data allow for quantitative micro-analyses of the issues surrounding pay competitiveness and quality of S/Es and allow for measures of workforce quality and performance based on the tracking of individuals over their DoD careers.

The first analyses presented in this report examine whether returns to skills[1] rose in the DoD labs as they did in the private sector. The next analyses focus on what, if any, changes in personnel outcomes that were observed in DoD labs over this period may have been caused by a lack of pay competitiveness. More precisely, did the DoD have greater difficulty in attracting and retaining high-quality S/Es over the study period than it had in the past?

---

[1]See Chapter Two for a discussion of returns to skills.

This report also examines whether personnel outcomes for S/Es were affected by the defense drawdown in the 1990s. Finally, the report analyzes whether personnel outcomes differed among the three pay systems: the General Schedule (GS), Performance Management Recognition System (PMRS), and experimental China Lake systems.

These analyses show that returns to measured or unmeasured skills declined slightly in the GS pay plan and were flat or increased only slightly in the PMRS and China Lake pay plans (this was especially true for the PMRS plan). In stark contrast to these findings, significant increases in returns to skills have occurred in the private sector. The lack of a similar change in returns to skills within the DoD is likely due to the centralized and rigid pay systems employed by the DoD (and the federal government as a whole). This would seem to suggest that the DoD may indeed have experienced increasing difficulty attracting and retaining quality S/E personnel over the study period. However, the study found little evidence that the quality of S/E personnel declined over time.

This study employed new measures of quality, including the performance of new hires relative to incumbents and the performance of those who eventually leave relative to those who stay with the DoD. There is little evidence to indicate a consistent trend over the study period in the performance of new hires relative to incumbents, suggesting that later new hires were not of relatively lower quality than earlier hires. Similarly, there exists no discernible trend in the performance of those who leave relative to those who stay with the DoD, suggesting no decline in the retention of high-quality S/Es.

Whereas these two sets of results may seem incompatible, they nevertheless may be compatible given that the private-sector defense industry was also hit hard by downsizing during this period. The availability of private-sector alternatives for scientific and engineering personnel with *defense-industry-specific* human capital probably did not increase as much as private-sector opportunities for other kinds of highly skilled workers. Although this explanation seems plausible, testing it further is beyond the scope of this study.

Finally, this report finds little evidence that any of the pay plans studied (GS, PMRS, and China Lake) resulted in changes for the better or worse in the quality of scientific and engineering personnel.

Under all three plans, the quality of these employees followed no apparent trend over time. Therefore, whereas the PMRS and China Lake plans may have a number of attractive features, they do not appear to noticeably improve the quality of the DoD's technical workforce when compared with the GS plan.

ACKNOWLEDGMENTS

I am indebted to RAND colleagues Beth Asch, Sue Hosek, and Al Robbert for their support, patience, and very constructive criticism. Rachel Louie provided invaluable assistance in assembling the necessary data sets, as did the DMDC's Debbie Eitelberg. Nancy DelFavero provided expert editorial help.

Diane Disney, Deputy Assistant Secretary of Defense for Civilian Personnel Policy, offered valuable guidance during the course of my research. Others on her staff, including Larry Lacy and John Nestor, were also very helpful.

Reviewers Jim Hosek and Carole Gresenz made exceptionally helpful suggestions for which I am grateful. Any remaining errors are, of course, my own.

DMDC	Defense Manpower Data Center
DoD	Department of Defense
FEPCA	Federal Employees Pay Comparability Act
GS	General Schedule
NSF	National Science Foundation
OCS	Occupational Compensation Survey
OPM	U.S. Office of Personnel Management
PATC	Professional, Administrative, Technical, and Clerical Pay Survey
PMRS	Performance Management Recognition System
S/Es	Scientists and Engineers
UICs	Unit Identification Codes

Chapter One

INTRODUCTION

BACKGROUND

The quality of scientific and engineering personnel in the Department of Defense (DoD) is of great concern, as is the quality of employees within the federal government as a whole. In recent years, scientists and engineers (S/Es) in particular have become increasingly important to the DoD and federal government as technology has rapidly advanced. S/E personnel in the federal government are responsible for new basic and applied research and administering federal science policy. In the DoD, S/Es are responsible for development of modern information systems and weaponry that are at the heart of the modern armed forces.

Numerous advisory boards and special commissions have criticized federal and DoD personnel and compensation practices for being bureaucratic, slow, inflexible, and allowing managers too little discretion when they need to hire or retain key personnel. Federal pay levels are often said to be too low, and reward systems are frequently criticized for providing poor incentives.

These concerns have existed for many years. Campbell and Dix (1990), in a report on personnel management of federal government scientists and engineers, concluded that, "Perceptions about factors affecting the federal government's ability to recruit and retain scientists and engineers have remained basically the same for the past 30 years, in spite of specific efforts by OPM and individual federal agencies to enhance such recruitment and retention."

1

Many attempts have been made over the years to solve these perceived problems. The Office of Personnel Management (OPM) has experimented with various changes to personnel systems, including special compensation rates (offered for most engineers since as early as 1955), outsourcing, and demonstration projects, such as the widely studied China Lake pay plan (this plan is described in Chapter Two). Various laws have been proposed over the years to add flexibility to pay plans and other systems, including the 1990 Federal Employees Pay Comparability Act (FEPCA).

S/Es are among the most skilled employees in the DoD's workforce, responsible for designing and developing the advanced systems and weapons that are so essential to today's armed forces. It is therefore of critical importance that the DoD is able to attract, develop, and retain highly skilled scientists and engineers, especially in its laboratories.

Moreover, there are several reasons why there may be greater concern about these issues now than in the past. The DoD's mission gradually changed after the cold war. This was coupled with the DoD's growing reliance on high technology, which increased the importance of having a qualified scientific and engineering staff. At the same time, the DoD underwent a substantial drawdown, decreasing its ranks through attrition, hiring freezes, and retirement incentives. These staff reductions can potentially make scientific and engineering careers within the DoD less attractive because of the possibility of fewer or slower promotion opportunities rates now and in the future.

Concurrent with these developments in the DoD, the private-sector economy was booming, driven in large part by technological advances (especially information technology). This transformed wage structures such that pay for highly skilled workers grew at a markedly greater rate than pay for other workers. Therefore, private-sector opportunities for highly skilled DoD S/Es may have grown, putting greater pressure on the DoD's ability to attract and retain qualified personnel.

OBJECTIVES

The purpose of this study is to examine the competitiveness of federal pay for civilian scientific and engineering personnel working in DoD laboratories from 1982 through 1996. Initial analyses in this study examine whether compensation rose as a function of employee skills in DoD labs, as it did in the private sector. Subsequent analyses focus on what, if any, changes in personnel outcomes observed in DoD labs over this period may have been caused by a lack of pay competitiveness. More precisely, did the DoD experience greater difficulty attracting and retaining high-quality S/Es over this period?

The study also examines whether personnel outcomes for S/Es were affected by the defense drawdown in the 1990s. Finally, the study analyzes whether personnel outcomes differed under three pay systems: the General Schedule (GS), Performance Management Recognition System (PMRS), and the experimental China Lake system.

APPROACH

This study uses longitudinal microdata from DoD personnel records to get a view of compensation and personnel outcomes for individuals in DoD labs. The study therefore complements prior research that used other types of empirical information and provides quantitative information that informs the debate over the DoD's ability to attract and retain highly skilled workers.

The study differs from prior research in that it focuses on *trends* in quality and outcomes of DoD personnel. The overall pay competitiveness of DoD jobs is difficult to assess, especially when using data available from the Department of Defense, which do not include information on private-sector opportunities. However, we can measure *changes* in the wage structure and returns to skills of DoD employees and compare them to the extensive literature on changes in private-sector wage structures. Similarly, quality of workers is difficult to assess objectively beyond using simple measures such as educational attainment. Nevertheless, changes over time in such quality measures can provide useful information on whether the DoD's ability to attract a high-quality workforce is deteriorating, as has often been claimed.

ORGANIZATION OF THIS REPORT

Chapter Two provides a review of relevant literature and the data used for this study. Chapter Three presents findings regarding compensation for education and other skills in the DoD laboratory workforce. Chapter Four examines quality trends among new recruits to the workforce. Chapter Five contrasts the quality of those who stay in the DoD workforce and those who choose to leave it. Chapter Six presents conclusions from this study.

Chapter Two

LITERATURE SURVEY AND DATA

Very little literature exists on the compensation of scientists and engineers working within the federal government, let alone within the DoD (see Campbell and Dix [1990] and the report's literature review appendix). Some previous studies used highly aggregated data published by federal agencies, such as the National Science Foundation (NSF). Other studies have used surveys, interviews, and field research on managers and personnel specialists working within government agencies.

These previous studies are useful for assessing S/E attitudes and subjective aspects of workforce quality. However, they lack quantitative information; therefore, it is difficult to get a sense of the degree to which the federal government or DoD has a problem with recruiting and retaining highly skilled workers. Furthermore, none of the studies present much information on trends in the quality of the technical workforce in the federal government. Instead, the studies focus on the overall level of pay. Because workforce quality is difficult to gauge with subjective data, information on quality trends might have been especially revealing.

LITERATURE ON PAY COMPARABILITY

Most of the literature on government worker pay focuses on the federal–private-sector "pay gap" between overall pay levels for comparable federal and private workers (few studies consider benefits because benefits data are not usually available). Most studies conclude that federal workers tend to be paid more than comparable private-sector workers, although some disagreement exists on the subject (Congressional Budget Office, 1997). Moulton (1990) found that federal administrative and professional workers had pay almost exactly comparable to that of their private-sector counterparts in 1988. He also found that federal pay was falling relative to the private sector in the 1980s. No systematic study has been done of later data, so no information exists on whether the trend continued into the 1990s.

Scant data on the pay of federal scientists and engineers are published, and data focused on the DoD are especially limited. Nevertheless, some rough indicators are available from NSF reports. Figures 2.1 and 2.2 plot mean salaries of recent B.A. and M.A. graduates in science and engineering from 1982 to 1993. These data suggest that private-sector engineers with a B.A. or M.A. tend to earn a little more than engineers in the federal government. No trend appears in the differences, suggesting that the federal government did not fall farther behind the private sector in salary levels over the sample period.

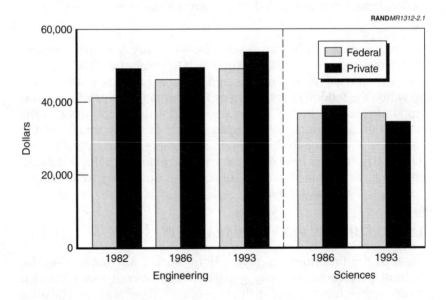

Figure 2.1—Mean Salaries of Recent Science and Engineering B.A.'s Employed in the Federal and Private Sectors

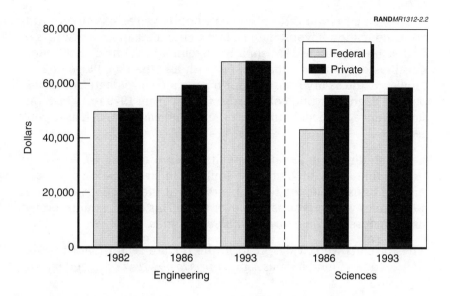

RAND*MR1312-2.2*

**Figure 2.2—Mean Salaries of Recent Science and Engineering M.A.'s
Employed in the Federal and Private Sectors**

One of the most important literatures in labor economics—how the
relationship between pay and skills has changed in recent decades—
applies to the present study. Many researchers have documented
important changes in the structure of labor market wages in the
1980s and 1990s (see, for example, Bound and Johnson, 1992; Juhn,
Murphy, and Pierce, 1993; Katz and Murphy, 1992; Murphy and
Welch, 1992; O'Shaughnessy, Levine, and Cappelli, 1998; and the
surveys by Levy and Murname, 1992, and Gottschalk and Danzinger,
1993). Specifically, the labor market returns to various measures of
skills[1] increased dramatically.

---

[1]*Returns to skills* is a standard term used in labor economics. It is based on the idea
that employees and firms invest in worker skills, or human capital, to increase productivity. This is done through increased education and on-the-job training. Returns
on the skills investments are shared by the employee (through higher earnings) and
the firm (through higher productivity, beyond the cost of higher earnings). The returns
to skills analyzed in this report are only the returns to the employee.

Figure 2.3 plots the ratio of median hourly wages of workers with some education beyond high school to the median hourly wages of high school graduates (Mishel, Bernstein, and Schmitt, 1997). Real earnings did not grow for workers with less than a college degree. However, the salary premium for having a college degree or an advanced degree beyond college rose sharply from 1979 to 1995. Similar evidence has been found for other skill measures, such as experience.

Other studies found that inequality in earnings increased within groups that are observationally similar (similar education or experience). For example, the ratio of earnings at the ninetieth and tenth percentiles within groups rose over time. This has been interpreted as an increase in the *return to unobserved skills.*

These trends were widespread in the private-sector labor market. Some studies found increases in *returns to observed skills* and *returns*

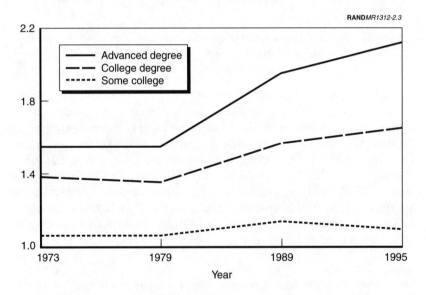

Figure 2.3—Ratio of Median Hourly Wages by Educational Attainment to Wages of High School Graduates, All U.S. Workers

to unobserved skills[2] within and between occupations, firms, establishments, and industries, and within demographic groups. These findings on increasing dispersion to skill investments have also been extended to the managerial ranks.

Katz and Krueger (1991) examined whether these private-sector trends were matched in the government sector. Using data from the Office of Personnel Management and other sources, they found that the public-sector college-degree wage premium remained fairly stable over the 1980s, unlike in the private sector. Similarly, they found that although job queues (waiting lists for government jobs) rose for government blue-collar jobs they fell for government white-collar jobs. Katz and Krueger hypothesized that their findings are the result of rigid government pay systems. However, they did not provide evidence on whether this affected the quality of the federal government's workforce.

One study, focusing on engineers, used data from the Professional, Administrative, Technical and Clerical Pay Survey (PATC; now called the Occupational Compensation Survey or OCS) conducted by the Department of Labor (Ferrall, 1995). The PATC surveyed firms about the compensation and level of responsibility of employees in various occupations. Ferrall found that the dispersion in earnings for engineers, across levels of responsibility, rose throughout 1985. Indeed, this is exactly what would be expected. If returns to skills are increasing, and firms place workers with higher skills in jobs with greater responsibility, then earnings should increase at higher levels relative to lower levels.

Figure 2.4 illustrates Ferrall's findings and extends them through 1995 (the sample employed in this study ends at the beginning of fiscal year 1996). The figure plots PATC data on median annual salaries

---

[2]A distinction is made in this report between "observed" and "unobserved" skills. *Observed skills* are those skills that are measured, or reasonably proxied, by variables in the employee data. These include educational attainment and years of service. *Unobserved skills* are those skills that must be inferred. To do so, it is assumed (as is standard in labor economics) that an employee's pay primarily reflects the economic value of his or her skills. Any variation in pay that is not explained by observed skills is presumed to be caused by unobserved skills.

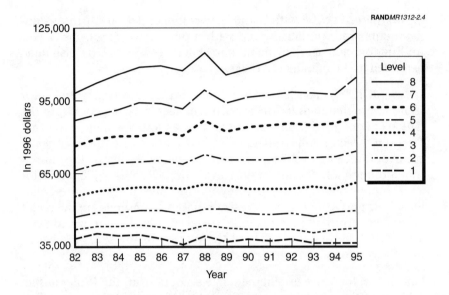

**Figure 2.4—Median Annual Salary of Private-Sector Engineers
by Level of Responsibility**

of private-sector engineers for different levels of responsibility over time.[3] The average percentage spread between pay at different levels rose in most years, especially after 1989. Therefore, not only do engineers tend to earn more now because they are in a highly skilled occupation, engineers with greater skills earn more now relative to engineers with lower skills. The same is likely to be true for other scientists and technical workers.

There is considerable debate over the causes of these changes in private-sector wage structures. One possible cause is an increase in international trade, which may diminish the earnings of blue-collar workers. Most authors suggest that the most significant cause is skill-biased technological change. New technology in the workplace has apparently resulted in increased demand for workers with higher skill levels. This explanation suggests an important reason why the DoD should be concerned about difficulties in attracting and retain-

---

[3]A few points are interpolated due to missing data.

ing highly skilled workers. These changes are most likely to affect the exact group studied in this report: highly skilled workers with science and engineering backgrounds who work in settings (such as laboratories) that make substantial use of new technology.

Moreover, as suggested by Katz and Krueger, and others who have written about federal pay systems, the DoD's pay and personnel systems are indeed rigid compared with those in the private sector. This makes it even more difficult for managers at DoD labs to attract and retain key technical workers.

One lesson learned from these studies on wage structures, and from the theoretical literature on personnel economics (Lazear, 1998), is that the earlier studies' focus on the overall level of pay is inadequate. Although it is important to know whether federal workers tend to be overpaid or underpaid, it is not the whole story. Changes in private-sector wage structures have been complex. Some classes of workers experienced declining earnings while others experienced substantial increases. As the PATC data suggest, even within occupational or other groups, changes have not been uniform. These changes are also likely to affect workers differentially at different stages of their careers.

From the DoD's perspective, it is important to examine pay comparability across workers' educational levels, experience, occupations, and levels of responsibility. In other words, achieving pay comparability is not simply a matter of determining a single pay level, but involves structuring a *system* that rewards workers differently depending on the value of their respective skills. This is one reason why the personnel data employed here are useful—they allow for examination of the structure of the entire pay system.

OVERVIEW OF STUDY DATA

The dataset used in this study was constructed from personnel records provided by the Defense Manpower Data Center (DMDC) to RAND. DMDC produced files with a snapshot of personnel information for all DoD civilian employees at the beginning of fiscal years

(October 1 of each year) 1982 through 1996. Temporary, seasonal, part-time, and inactive workers were excluded from these data.[4]

Records used in the analysis were for those employees classified as a scientist, engineer (but not civil engineer), or mathematician according to the DoD's Functional Occupational Group.[5] To maintain a focus on skilled workers, those workers with less than a bachelor's degree were excluded. Finally, the DMDC provided a list of Unit Identification Codes (UICs) for DoD labs, which were matched to the sample to identify lab employees.

The DMDC provided a large variety of variables for each employee each year. Demographic variables include age, race, gender, handicapped status, veteran status, and region and census district of employment. Job variables include the agency (Army, Navy, or other), the bureau within each agency, the unit identification code, several functional and occupational codes, supervisory or managerial status, and years of service.[6] Compensation variables include salary, pay plan, pay grade, last performance rating, eligibility for any special pay adjustments, and type of retirement plan. Therefore, the study is limited to analyzing annual salary rather than the monetary value of benefits.

The data also provide information on whether the employee is a new hire or will exit the DoD in the fiscal year.[7] Exits were classified into retirements and separations using DMDC transaction codes. Promotions were defined as increases in salary grade (if the employee stayed in the same pay plan) between years.

------

[4]A 20 percent random sample of this base dataset is used by Asch and Warner (1999).

[5]MOG-FOG codes 10, 11, and 20.

[6]The years of service variable was nonsequential from year to year for some employees (most were in the Air Force Materiel Command or were veterans; see Asch and Warner [1999], Appendix B). These observations were excluded from analyses involving years of service. Alternative specifications for years of service were tried with no difference in empirical inferences.

[7]New hires may be rehires or have prior experience with some federal agency. In some cases, it is possible that a new hire previously worked at the same DoD lab, for example, but as an employee for the Department of Energy. It is impossible to identify such cases, or how frequent they are. One implication of rehires is that years of service can be greater than zero for a new hire.

Educational attainment and academic discipline of the employee's last degree were provided. However, according to the DMDC, the education variable is not always updated when an individual acquires more education. It is not known how often DoD lab S/Es acquire additional education while employed at the DoD. Thus, the education variable provides at least the employee's level of education, and the academic discipline of the employee's highest academic degree, upon hiring.

Table 2.1 presents summary statistics. The sample is roughly 90 percent male and 85 percent white, with both proportions declining over the period. Average age and years of service crept up over the second half of the period. As will be seen later in this chapter, this was caused by the manner in which the DoD implemented the drawdown during the 1990s. More than half of those in the sample were employed by the Navy, about a third by the Army, and the remainder by the Air Force. Almost no lab employees worked for agencies in the "fourth estate" (DoD agencies outside of the military services), and none for the Marines.[8] About 10 percent of lab employees had a Ph.D. or law or medical degree; about 25 percent an M.A.[9] The table shows academic disciplines of the last degrees recorded. About 75 percent had an engineering degree (other than civil engineering). Math and physics constituted an important but declining fraction of the sample, down to 15 percent by 1994. About 3 percent had their most recent recorded degree in business.

Although most lab employees were in the GS pay plan, a large fraction were in two other plans, PMRS and China Lake. These plans were intended to provide greater flexibility in pay, so it is interesting to compare the effects of the three plans in the analyses that follow.

N in all tables denotes sample sizes.

---

[8]The fourth estate has no DoD labs. The small number of employees in the fourth estate and working in a DoD lab were presumably assigned to a lab run by a military service.

[9]The education variable was coded with M.D.'s and law degrees lumped together with Ph.D.'s. This is unlikely to make much difference for this study. Both groups should earn more than an M.A. Moreover, there should be very few lawyers or doctors (judging from the fraction of the sample classified with a medical academic discipline) in the sample of DoD lab scientists and engineers.

Table 2.1

Summary Statistics

		1982	1989	1996
Female		5%	9%	11%
Race	Black	3%	3%	3%
	Hispanic	2%	3%	4%
	White	92%	87%	84%
	Other	4%	7%	9%
Age (mean)		42.4	41.5	43.8
Education	B.A.	63%	67%	62%
	M.A.	26%	23%	28%
	Ph.D., M.D., or law	11%	10%	10%
Academic discipline	Biology	2%	2%	2%
	Business	3%	3%	3%
	Computer science	1%	1%	2%
	Engineering	65%	74%	76%
	Medicine	0%	0%	0%
	Math/statistics	9%	6%	5%
	Physics	17%	12%	10%
	Chemistry	2%	1%	1%
	Astronomy	0%	0%	0%
	Geology	1%	1%	1%
Agency	Army	33%	32%	33%
	Navy	53%	56%	55%
	Air Force	13%	12%	12%
	Fourth estate	0%	1%	1%
Years of service (mean)		15.6	14.3	16.5
Annual salary (mean)		$55,394	$53,694	$57,432
Pay plan	GS	95%	68%	68%
	PMRS	0%	23%	19%
	China Lake	0%	8%	12%
	Other	5%	1%	1%
N		32,721	43,472	41,287

NOTES: Academic disciplines are for 1994 in the last column, as that is the last available year for this variable. Annual salary means are in constant (1996) dollars.

About 20 percent were paid for part of the period under the PMRS, which was designed to provide greater recognition and incentives than the GS system. It covered federal managers in Grades 13 through 15. The system affected the way that within-grade pay raises were determined. Rather than receiving step increases based on time within a grade, employees competed for merit increases based on performance evaluations (Mace and Yoder, 1995). PMRS was technically in effect through 1993 but in practice persisted through the end of the sample period (the start of fiscal year 1996) because PMRS employees were off-step compared with GS employees when the pay plan ended. After that, they remained off-step, receiving the same time-in-grade–based step increases that they would have received under the GS plan. Employees were gradually switched back to the GS plan when they were promoted, demoted, transferred to another agency, or had a break in service.

The Navy instituted an experimental pay plan at the Naval Weapons Center at China Lake, California, during the period; this plan covered 12 percent of sampled employees by 1996. At China Lake, a number of flexibilities in personnel management were implemented, including a dual-career ladder in which technical workers were promoted based on technical skills and could earn more than their managers. Importantly, China Lake is a broadband plan, with only five primary pay grades (as opposed to 15 under the GS plan). Broadband plans are often advocated as a way of providing more flexible salary growth and incentives than traditional salary band plans. More flexible salary growth could conceivably allow the DoD to attract and retain quality lab personnel better than the conventional civil service model would. The U.S. Office of Personnel Management (OPM) reported some initial success with the plan, including an improvement in quality of hires as measured by managerial perceptions, and increases in grade point average of recruits (Office of Personnel Management, 1986).

Average salary (in constant 1996 dollars) increased in the second half of the period. This is not because of changes in DoD salary structures. For example, most of the sampled employees were paid under the GS pay plan, the primary pay plan for all federal civilian employees. The GS pay plan did not change in structure (relative pay across salary grades) during the entire period.[10] Instead, the federal gov-

---

[10]This is in sharp contrast to the structure of pay across responsibility levels for engineers in the private sector, as in the example in Figure 2.4. This is evidence of the rigidity of federal pay plans relative to pay in the private sector.

ernment merely awarded across-the-board percentage salary increases each year and, if anything, these increases slightly trailed increases in the private sector from 1982 through 1996. The same was true for salary raises across grades in the PMRS and China Lake pay plans. The average salary increased in this sample because the DoD had increasing percentages of lab personnel (indeed, of all DoD civilian personnel) in higher salary grades in later years. This was caused by the way in which the DoD implemented the drawdown, as discussed later in this section.

Figure 2.5 shows the total number of DoD S/E lab employees over the period 1982 through 1996. Figure 2.6 breaks down employees by new hires, separations, and retirements. For example, about 7 percent of employees in 1982 were new hires, about 1 percent would retire that year, and about 3 percent would separate. Separations and retirements are plotted as negative numbers because they represent outflows from the workforce. Therefore, summing all types of outflows plus new hires gives a rough idea of the total percentage change in the sample.

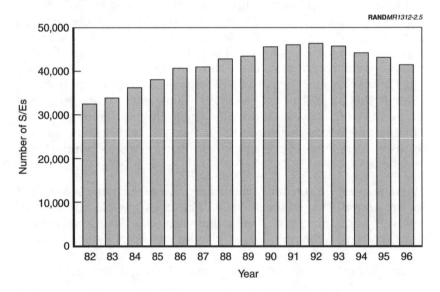

Figure 2.5—Sample Size

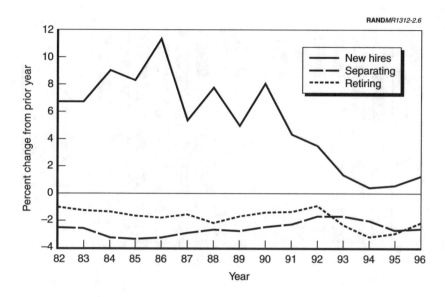

Figure 2.6—S/E Workforce Flows

The sample size fell from 1992 through 1996. This is due in part to an increase in retirements from 1993 onward. The DoD began a major drawdown at the end of fiscal year 1989, decreasing its labor force through attrition, hiring freezes, and early retirement incentives. Mitigating the rise in retirements, separations declined from about 1985 to 1992. However, the main reason for the decline in worker population is that hiring fell dramatically after 1990 during the drawdown to almost zero by 1994.

Figure 2.7 shows how S/Es were distributed across pay grades (for those in the GS pay system). Almost all employees were in Grades 11 and higher.[11] The grade distribution was relatively stable in the first half of the sample period, with 20 percent of lab employees in Grades 6 through 11. Starting around 1990 during the drawdown, the proportion in Grades 6 through 11 dropped dramatically. This was caused by hiring freezes combined with a disproportionate concen-

---

[11]Promotion rates for lab S/Es out of Grades 1 through 10 are very high.

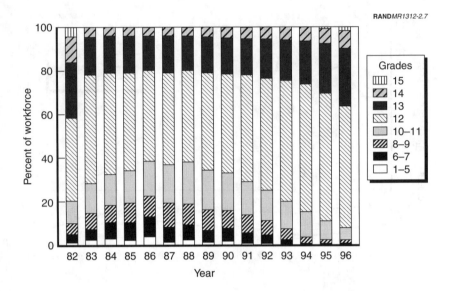

Figure 2.7—Distribution of S/Es Across GS Grades

tration of reductions in lower-grade positions. Inflows to lower grades dropped off while incumbents in those grades kept moving to higher grades.

A net result of the drawdown was to make the DoD S/E workforce top-heavy in salary grades over time. Because data on job duties are unavailable, it is not clear whether this reflects any change in job responsibilities of technical workers. In fact, given the hiring freezes, it is likely that many labs simply kept technical workers in their current duties but promoted them to higher salary grades in order to retain them and offer expected salary increases. In this sense, it may be that the DoD increased its compensation cost for similar work over the period, although it is impossible to state this with certainty given the dataset.

This top-heavy structure implies that the DoD may have problems recruiting workers in the future if it decides to increase hiring. Top-heavy upper grades might slow promotion rates for two reasons. First, if the DoD adjusts the distribution of employees across grades to return to a greater percentage representation in lower grades, it will have to hire disproportionately more workers into the lower ranks. Upper positions will already be filled, implying poor future promotion opportunities for new hires compared with the very high historical promotion rates out of lower grades in the past. Second, as seen in Figure 2.8, the age distribution of the S/E workforce shifted toward workers in their 30s. These workers still have long careers ahead of them; therefore, the bulge in the upper ranks is unlikely to be effectively trimmed through attrition, assuming current policy prevails.

Another potential problem with these changes in the demographics and grade distribution of S/Es is that the current workforce may not be as up to date on recent technological advances as would be desirable for the DoD. New hires and recent graduates are more likely to e familiar with the latest advances in technology. Although these issues are interesting and may cause concern regarding potential quality problems in the DoD S/E workforce, they are beyond the scope of this study and therefore not addressed in this report.

RAND*MR1312-2.8*

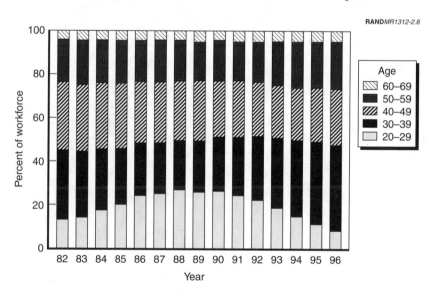

Figure 2.8—Age Distribution

Chapter Three

RETURNS TO EDUCATION AND UNOBSERVED SKILLS

This chapter analyzes one of the key questions posed in this report: Did the earnings premium for highly skilled workers in the DoD rise over the sample period 1982 through 1996?

In this chapter, changes in returns to skills among DoD lab personnel are analyzed in order to compare them with changes in returns to skills in the private sector. Following the labor economics literature, returns to two types of skills are analyzed: observed skills, such as education and years of service, and unobserved skills. Returns to unobserved skills are inferred by looking at dispersion in earnings for employees after controlling for observed skills and other factors such as pay plan. Any remaining dispersion in earnings should reflect skills other than those already controlled for.

The basic findings show that returns to skills decreased for GS employees, rose a little but not systematically for PMRS employees, and declined or stayed flat for China Lake employees over 1982 through 1996. For lab employees as a whole, returns to skills fell or did not rise as consistently or as markedly as they did in the private sector.

RETURNS TO EDUCATION

The first approach to measuring returns to skills is to employ the classic earnings function from labor economics. Salary is regressed on control variables that might affect an individual's earnings for reasons other than the employee's skills and measures of skills that the labor market rewards. Table 3.1 illustrates this method by presenting earnings regressions for the three pay plans discussed in

Table 3.1

Returns to Education and Experience

	Dependent Variable: log(Annual Salary in 1996 $)		
	GS	PMRS	China Lake
Intercept	10.502***	10.870***	10.537***
M.A.	0.064***	0.040***	0.058***
Ph.D., M.D., or law	0.228***	0.131***	0.184***
Years of service	0.039***	0.015***	0.036***
Years of service^2	0.001***	0.000***	0.001***
Scientist	0.090***	0.003***	0.038***
Mathematician	0.082***	0.012***	0.019***
Army	0.011***	0.010***	—
Navy	0.043***	0.057***	—
R^2	0.65	0.38	0.64
N	386,733	118,753	41,833

NOTES: ***= significant at 1%; **= at 5%; *= at 10%.

Chapter Two. The dependent variable is the log of annual salary; therefore, coefficients can be interpreted as the percentage effect of the variable on salary. Thus, coefficients on skill variables represent returns to those skills.

The skill measures analyzed are education (dummy variables for whether the employee's last reported degree is an M.A. or Ph.D.) and on-the-job experience measured as years of service with the DoD. All regressions in Tables 3.1 through 3.4 include controls for race, gender, veteran status, region, and agency.

The regression results are similar to those of most earnings function regressions. A master's degree implies higher annual earnings of about 6 percent, whereas a Ph.D., M.D., or law degree implies higher annual earnings of about 20 percent. Greater on-the-job experience, measured by years of service, also implies higher earnings. For example, an employee with five years of service earns about 20 percent more than a new hire, everything else being equal.

Note that returns to skill measures discussed here and in the rest of this report are the result of two factors: variation in earnings within jobs and mobility across jobs. For example, a typical engineer with an M.A. might earn more than a typical engineer with a B.A. both because higher skills place him or her in a higher salary grade and because of promotion to higher ranks over his or her career.

Changes in returns to skills measured over time therefore include the effects of several DoD policies: overall pay levels across grades, grades at which hiring occurs, rates of movement between salary steps within grades, and rates of promotion across grades. In practice, relative pay levels across grades did not change over the observed period in any of the pay plans. Therefore, returns to skills reflect differences in grades at hiring and mobility within and between grades.

R^2s are high compared with typical earnings regressions. This is due to DoD personnel policies. In the GS plan, compensation is rigidly attached to salary grade and step within the grade, and promotions are more closely associated with employee job tenure, than in most private-sector organizations.[1] While pay varies less with step and more with performance in the PMRS and China Lake pay plans, it still is more closely linked to salary grade and seniority than in the private sector.

For many analyses in this report, especially for the GS pay plan, sample sizes are very large, in which case t-statistics and statistical significances are not very informative. The economic significance of the coefficient estimate is more helpful in such cases. In presenting the information in the tables in this chapter, the emphasis is not so much on the levels of coefficients as it is on the *trends* in the coefficients over time. Therefore, Tables 3.2 through 3.4 report only the coefficients on skill measures for various years.

For each pay plan, regressions of the form shown in Table 3.1 were run for each available year by subsamples of the three most common academic disciplines or occupations (other disciplines or occupations covered relatively small percentages of the sample). Coefficients for education dummy variables are reported for every other year to examine trends in returns to observed skills. Coefficients are normalized to equal 1 in 1982 in order to make analysis of trends more transparent. Table 3.2 reports results for GS employees, Table 3.3 for PMRS employees, and Table 3.4 for China Lake employees.

---

[1]Earnings regressions including salary grade dummies yield R^2s well above .9; earnings regressions including salary step dummies yield R^2s of about .99 for GS employees. Thus, almost all variation in earnings for S/Es is due to hiring or promotion into different grades, plus merit increases for PMRS employees.

Table 3.2

Returns to Education over Time, GS Pay Plan

	Academic Discipline					
	Engineering		Math and Statistics		Physics	
	M.A.	Ph.D.	M.A.	Ph.D.	M.A.	Ph.D.
1982	1.00***	1.00***	1.00***	1.00***	1.00***	1.00***
1984	1.01***	1.00***	1.07***	1.10***	1.35***	1.06***
1986	1.09***	1.09***	1.03***	1.26***	1.36***	1.05***
1988	1.00***	0.89***	0.85***	0.96***	1.39***	1.03***
1990	0.92***	0.88***	0.67***	0.84***	1.39***	1.06***
1992	0.70***	0.81***	0.83***	0.85***	1.10***	0.94***
1994	0.56***	0.66***	0.78***	0.77***	0.91***	0.86***
N: 1982	15,479		2,083		3,814	
N: 1994	19,491		1,146		1,911	

	Occupation					
	Engineer		Mathematician		Scientist	
	M.A.	Ph.D.	M.A.	Ph.D.	M.A.	Ph.D.
1982	1.00***	1.00***	1.00***	1.00***	1.00***	1.00***
1984	0.92***	0.97***	0.97***	1.04***	1.15***	1.02***
1986	1.06***	1.07***	0.92***	1.01***	1.08***	1.00***
1988	0.97***	0.90***	0.81***	0.85***	1.16***	1.00***
1990	0.89***	0.90***	0.63***	0.76***	1.07***	1.01***
1992	0.71***	0.82***	0.80***	0.73***	1.17***	1.01***
1994	0.59***	0.69***	0.71***	0.67***	0.93***	0.89***
1996	0.56***	0.70***	0.64***	0.57***	0.95***	0.91***
N: 1982	18,112		2,581		5,667	
N: 1996	21,227		1,522		3,279	

NOTES: ***= significant at 1%; **= at 5%; *= at 10%. Statistics are coefficients on education dummy variables from earnings regressions similar to those in Table 3.1, normalized relative to the coefficient in the 1982 regression.

Analyses focus on education measures; results for years of service were similar.

For GS employees, a clear pattern emerges from Table 3.2. Returns to education declined for both M.A.'s and Ph.D.'s during the sample period. In many cases, returns appear to have increased for the first two years, although it is possible that this pattern is an artifact of spottier data at the beginning of the sample. After that, in most cases returns to education fell consistently for most of the period. The general decline in education premiums holds for the three primary academic disciplines, as well as for the three primary occupational

Table 3.3

Returns to Education over Time, PMRS Pay Plan

| | Academic Discipline | | | | | |
| | Engineering | | Math and Statistics | | Physics | |
	M.A.	Ph.D.	M.A.	Ph.D.	M.A.	Ph.D.
1983	1.00***	1.00***	1.00***	1.00***	1.00***	1.00***
1984	0.91***	0.91***	0.89***	1.02***	0.68***	0.85***
1986	1.01***	1.00***	1.02***	1.14***	0.74***	1.05***
1988	1.29***	1.03***	0.81***	1.06***	0.63***	0.92***
1990	1.43***	1.17***	0.74***	1.12***	0.82***	1.05***
1992	1.51***	1.17***	0.64***	1.15***	0.63***	1.06***
1994	1.67***	1.12***	0.50***	0.96***	0.64**	0.91***
N: 1983	2,618		274		512	
N: 1994	5,897		545		1,222	

| | Occupation | | | | | |
| | Engineer | | Mathematician | | Scientist | |
	M.A.	Ph.D.	M.A.	Ph.D.	M.A.	Ph.D.
1983	1.00***	1.00***	1.00***	1.00***	1.00	1.00***
1984	0.79***	0.87***	0.70*	0.70***	1.01***	1.01***
1986	0.86***	0.97***	1.33***	0.95***	1.12***	1.25***
1988	0.94***	1.00***	1.78***	0.86***	1.17***	1.19***
1990	1.02***	1.06***	1.45***	0.84***	1.31***	1.33***
1992	1.09***	1.06***	1.35***	0.85***	0.95***	1.29***
1994	1.16***	1.06***	1.61***	0.74***	1.03***	1.19***
1996	1.00***	1.05***	1.52***	0.71***	1.37***	1.23***
N: 1983	3,363		323		935	
N: 1996	5,204		480		1,447	

NOTES: ***= significant at 1%; **= at 5%; *= at 10%. Statistics are coefficients on education dummy variables from earnings regressions similar to those in Table 3.1, normalized relative to the coefficient in the 1982 regression.

groups. This pattern is surprising given that it is the opposite of what happened in the private sector.

Patterns in returns to education for PMRS employees are different from those for GS employees. In most cases, returns to education rose over the period, especially for those with an M.A. or engineering degree. Those with math and statistics or physics degrees experienced a decline in returns to their degrees. In contrast, those employed as mathematicians and scientists experienced a rise in returns to education. These returns did vary quite a bit from year to year due to smaller sample sizes for mathematicians, physicists, and

Table 3.4

Returns to Education over Time, China Lake Pay Plan

| | Academic Discipline | | | | | |
| | Engineering | | Math and Statistics | | Physics | |
	M.A.	Ph.D.	M.A.	Ph.D.	M.A.	Ph.D.
1986	1.00***	1.00***	1.00***	1.00***	1.00***	1.00***
1988	1.10***	1.05***	0.76**	0.86***	0.79***	0.98***
1990	1.07***	1.03***	0.99***	0.93***	0.94***	0.99***
1992	0.95***	0.97***	0.60	1.01***	0.87***	0.93***
1994	0.76***	0.95***	0.91**	0.75***	0.70**	0.86***
N: 1986	1,804		312		612	
N: 1994	3,184		313		521	

| | Academic Discipline | | | | | |
| | Engineer | | Mathematician | | Scientist | |
	M.A.	Ph.D.	M.A.	Ph.D.	M.A.	Ph.D.
1984	0.82***	0.81***	0.70***	0.40***	0.60***	0.83***
1986	1.00***	1.00***	1.00***	1.00***	1.00***	1.00***
1988	1.11***	1.09***	0.73***	0.96***	0.69***	0.90***
1990	1.06***	1.12***	0.88***	1.05***	0.83***	0.88***
1992	0.89***	1.01***	0.58***	0.90***	0.85***	0.86***
1994	0.77***	1.03***	0.62***	0.66***	0.79***	0.82***
1996	0.89***	0.75***	0.64***	0.30***	0.85***	0.72***
N: 1984	857		136		293	
N: 1996	3,816		382		475	

NOTES: ***= significant at 1%; **=at 5%; *= at 10%. Statistics are coefficients on education dummy variables from earnings regressions similar to those in Table 3.1, normalized relative to the coefficient in the 1982 regression.

scientists; therefore, it is difficult to discern a general pattern in returns to education except for engineers.

What does seem clear is that there is no general decline, and there is greater variation, in returns to schooling for PMRS employees. This probably reflects the design of the pay plan, which afforded some ability to reward according to level of performance instead of seniority. Although there are gains in returns to schooling, they are not as consistent nor as large as what was experienced in the private sector.

Sample sizes are particularly small in most cases for the China Lake pay plan throughout the report, so any inferences will be less precise for this pay plan. A pattern that does emerge appears to be similar to that for the GS plan: a general decline over time in returns to schooling for both M.A.'s and Ph.D.'s for all types of academic disciplines and occupations. Again, this is the opposite of what occurred in the private sector. The China Lake plan's greater similarity to the GS plan suggests that it may not afford the same opportunity to reward employees according to their level of performance as does the PMRS plan, although it is difficult to determine this with certainty given these data.

RETURNS TO UNOBSERVED SKILLS

In this section, returns to unobserved skills are analyzed using the method typically employed in the wage distribution literature. After controlling for observed skills (education and years of service), we examine the wage distribution over time to determine if the spread between low and high earners increases. If wages represent payment for observed and unobserved skills, the distribution of pay after controlling for observed skills provides evidence on the extent to which a pay premium exists for unobserved skills.

Tables 3.5 through 3.7 present the results of the analysis of returns to unobserved skills for the three pay plans. The tables show ratios of the ninetieth to tenth percentiles of the wage distribution over time. These ratios are calculated within categories (education, years of service, and occupation) to control for observed skills and other factors.

Tables 3.5 through 3.7 lump together employees with various years of service in order to present this information in a single table. A potential concern arising from clustering employee data in this way is that it might confound year-of-service effects with compositional effects (for example, because of the drop in hiring during the military drawdown of the 1990s). To address this, wage dispersion ratios were calculated for specific years of service for each of the groups analyzed in the tables.

For each pay plan, the statistic was regressed on years of service, fiscal years, education, and occupation (the regressions are not reported) to check the coefficient on fiscal year. The results confirm the findings discussed here. Fiscal year has a negative, statistically significant effect on wage dispersion for the GS plan and a positive effect for both the PMRS and China Lake plans, but is significant only

Table 3.5

Dispersion in Returns to Unobserved Skills, GS Pay Plan

		Years of Service							
		1–5			6–10			11+	
	B.A.	M.A.	Ph.D.	B.A.	M.A.	Ph.D.	B.A.	M.A.	Ph.D.
				Engineer					
1982	1.26	1.31	1.45	1.53	1.56	1.43	1.46	1.40	1.46
1984	1.23	1.27	1.41	1.41	1.36	1.48	1.75	1.41	1.39
1986	1.30	1.28	1.41	1.37	1.36	1.48	1.69	1.46	1.41
1988	1.28	1.26	1.36	1.32	1.33	1.40	1.46	1.42	1.41
1990	1.21	1.24	1.34	1.31	1.31	1.39	1.48	1.42	1.33
1992	1.20	1.19	1.32	1.29	1.33	1.41	1.55	1.42	1.42
1994	1.19	1.19	1.32	1.29	1.37	1.43	1.26	1.34	1.34
1996	1.17	1.19	1.29	1.29	1.41	1.45	1.34	1.34	1.33
N: 1982	1,732	491	144	9,186	3,265	426	1,604	314	95
N: 1996	5,604	1,405	166	8,354	3,333	403	1,127	369	170
				Mathematician					
1982	1.49	1.47	—	1.42	1.49	1.42	1.77	—	—
1984	1.45	1.43	—	1.37	1.41	1.57	1.77	—	—
1986	1.54	1.43	—	1.41	1.41	1.61	1.77	—	—
1988	1.43	1.34	—	1.41	1.41	1.52	1.77	—	—
1990	1.43	1.47	—	1.45	1.41	1.61	1.83	—	—
1992	1.23	1.31	—	1.43	1.36	1.48	1.83	—	—
1994	1.34	1.34	—	1.45	1.36	1.48	1.55	—	—
1996	1.38	1.23	—	1.36	1.45	1.61	1.28	—	—
N: 1982	213	120	—	1,056	593	111	229	—	—
N: 1996	194	73	—	644	424	75	51	—	—
				Scientist					
1982	1.64	1.62	1.49	1.68	1.62	1.42	1.89	1.60	1.52
1984	1.64	1.43	1.34	1.54	1.51	1.52	1.53	1.77	1.47
1986	1.54	1.43	1.26	1.54	1.51	1.52	1.77	1.64	1.51
1988	1.45	1.47	1.30	1.55	1.55	1.56	1.77	1.72	1.37
1990	1.44	1.47	1.32	1.59	1.58	1.52	1.83	1.60	1.39
1992	1.52	1.43	1.33	1.59	1.55	1.52	1.89	1.69	1.43
1994	1.63	1.46	1.36	1.59	1.49	1.53	1.86	1.58	1.36
1996	1.43	1.38	1.37	1.54	1.49	1.53	1.83	1.72	1.51
N: 1982	199	156	330	1,740	1,172	1,171	245	175	309
N: 1996	245	188	283	783	610	672	97	86	228

for the PMRS plan. For all three pay plans, the coefficients are small and economically insignificant.

Table 3.5 shows that, once again, trends in the pay structure for GS employees did not match those of the private sector. In virtually all cases, wage dispersion within groups declined, indicating a decline

Table 3.6

Dispersion in Returns to Unobserved Skills, PMRS Pay Plan

	Years of Service						
	1–5			6–10			11+
	B.A.	M.A.	Ph.D.	B.A.	M.A.	Ph.D.	Ph.D.
Engineer							
1983	1.27	1.46	1.29	1.40	1.43	1.38	—
1984	1.22	1.33	1.38	1.40	1.44	1.38	—
1986	1.18	1.33	1.37	1.45	1.47	1.42	—
1988	1.19	1.31	1.37	1.44	1.46	1.44	—
1990	1.22	1.28	1.40	1.40	1.43	1.47	—
1992	1.16	1.26	1.39	1.39	1.45	1.47	—
1994	1.16	1.25	1.41	1.41	1.45	1.45	—
1996	1.25	1.37	1.55	1.41	1.50	1.45	—
N: 1983	59	39	24	1,854	1,069	130	—
N: 1996	89	50	46	2,682	1,951	348	—
Mathematician							
1983	—	—	—	1.35	1.35	1.45	—
1984	—	—	—	1.36	1.36	1.49	—
1986	—	—	—	1.44	1.43	1.60	—
1988	—	—	—	1.40	1.43	1.49	—
1990	—	—	—	1.40	1.42	1.50	—
1992	—	—	—	1.38	1.42	1.46	—
1994	—	—	—	1.38	1.46	1.44	—
1996	—	—	—	1.37	1.48	1.44	—
N: 1983	—	—	—	146	120	32	—
N: 1996	—	—	—	199	210	57	—
Scientist							
1983	—	—	1.38	1.43	1.46	1.38	1.77
1984	—	—	1.41	1.45	1.45	1.41	1.56
1986	—	—	1.32	1.45	1.45	1.47	1.54
1988	—	—	1.37	1.47	1.43	1.49	1.56
1990	—	—	1.44	1.42	1.49	1.49	1.53
1992	—	—	1.40	1.47	1.50	1.48	1.48
1994	—	—	1.40	1.46	1.50	1.46	1.46
1996	—	—	1.40	1.51	1.53	1.47	1.46
N: 1983	—	—	69	251	202	346	28
N: 1996	—	—	106	248	323	712	30

in returns to unobserved skills for GS lab employees. In most cases, a significant drop in returns to unobserved skills is observed from 1982 to 1984. Although is not clear why this drop occurred, statistical analyses, in general, tend to be somewhat less robust with the earliest years of data. Therefore, this observation may be due to problems with the first year of data.

Table 3.7

Dispersion in Returns to Unobserved Skills, China Lake Pay Plan

	Years of Service						
	1–5		6–10			11+	
	B.A.	M.A.	B.A.	M.A.	Ph.D.	B.A.	M.A.
				Engineer			
1984	1.24	1.14	1.53	1.55	1.57	—	—
1986	1.45	1.33	1.49	1.53	1.47	1.33	1.60
1988	1.47	1.33	1.48	1.54	1.48	1.41	1.55
1990	1.40	1.34	1.52	1.52	1.51	1.47	1.67
1992	1.38	1.44	1.53	1.53	1.44	1.37	1.41
1994	1.24	1.37	1.50	1.58	1.41	1.28	1.26
1996	1.31	1.30	1.48	1.59	1.43	1.46	1.85
N: 1984	149	52	812	459	70	357	58
N: 1996	774	138	1,820	741	94	158	32
				Mathematician			
1984	1.47	—	1.40	1.46	1.41	—	—
1986	1.60	—	1.51	1.56	1.44	—	—
1988	1.53	—	1.56	1.56	1.40	—	—
1990	1.30	—	1.60	1.52	1.46	—	—
1992	1.40	—	1.74	1.55	1.39	—	—
1994	1.47	—	1.73	1.64	1.75	—	—
1996	1.55	—	1.79	1.67	1.82	—	—
N: 1984	28	—	118	81	24	—	—
N: 1996	38	—	161	118	26	—	—
				Scientist			
1984	1.30	—	1.59	1.52	1.67	—	—
1986	1.52	—	1.52	1.47	1.60	—	—
1988	1.53	—	1.54	1.44	1.54	—	—
1990	1.49	—	1.56	1.59	1.64	—	—
1992	1.33	—	1.72	1.60	1.56	—	—
1994	1.36	—	1.73	1.61	1.53	—	—
1996	1.46	—	1.54	1.61	1.52	—	—
N: 1984	26	—	144	125	120	—	—
N: 1996	42	—	125	130	119	—	—

Ignoring 1982, engineers, mathematicians, and scientists with few years of service experienced a decline in the average return to unobserved skills from 1984 through 1996. The trend was mixed for mathematicians and scientists with more years of service but generally remained flat. In any case, no trend toward an increase in returns to unobserved skills appears, unlike in the private sector where there is such a trend.

Results for PMRS employees are again different than those for GS employees. There is no general decline in unobserved skills for PMRS S/Es; instead, returns are generally flat or increase a little. Thus, the PMRS pay plan was better able to reward skills than the GS plan. However, increases in returns to unobserved skills are smaller than what was experienced in the private sector.[2]

Table 3.7 shows results for China Lake employees that are similar to those for PMRS employees. Returns to unobserved skills were flat or increased slightly in most cases, but had no clear pattern.

Based on the patterns found in Tables 3.2 through 3.7, we might expect a decline in the quality of GS S/Es over the period 1982 through 1996 because returns to all skill measures fell for that pay plan. We might expect a somewhat smaller decline in the quality of China Lake S/Es, and even less still for PMRS employees. This issue is examined in the next two chapters of this report.

---

[2]It should be noted, though, that the literature only looks at samples of employees across firms whereas the present study only considers changes within a single firm. It might be possible that returns to skills increase in the entire labor market but not within specific firms (for example, due to rigid salary structures).

Chapter Four

RECRUITMENT OF HIGH-QUALITY SCIENTISTS AND ENGINEERS

One approach to assessing pay comparability is to examine the extent to which the DoD experienced good or bad personnel outcomes that may be caused by relatively high or low pay. If pay is low or declining relative to the private sector, this may cause a decline in the quality of S/Es the DoD is able to recruit or retain. In this chapter, the quality of new S/E recruits is examined. In the next chapter, the quality of the S/Es the DoD retains is examined.

The quality of new recruits is difficult to measure. In this chapter and Chapter Five, two types of measures are used: human capital and on-the-job performance. For example, an academic degree is a measure of general human capital. Another measure of human capital is work experience, measured by age and years of service. Age proxies for total labor market experience, whereas years of service measure DoD-specific experience.

The panel structure of the dataset also allows for longitudinal measures of on-the-job performance. The first measure is the employee's performance rating, which is measured as a dummy variable indicating if the employee's most recent rating was the highest possible.[1] A second potential measure is the promotion experience of the employee. Because salary is so closely tied to grade in the DoD, salary growth is an equivalent but more straightforward measure of promotion experience that is employed here. Neither the performance

---

[1]Performance ratings are subjective evaluations by the employee's supervisor. The employee was rated on a scale of 1 to 5, with 1 being the best performance rating.

rating dummy variable nor salary growth is a perfect measure of quality. Nevertheless, it is hoped that the combined information from all of the measures will be useful in assessing the ability of the DoD to attract and retain high-quality S/Es.

Chapters Four and Five use a "difference-in-differences" approach. In this chapter, quality measures of new hires are compared with those of incumbent employees promoted into the same grade in the same pay plan in the same year. Trends in these relative measures are examined to determine if the DoD experienced any discernible decline in the relative quality or performance of new recruits. Similarly, Chapter Five looks for trends in the relative performance of those employees who exit the DoD compared with those employees the DoD retains.

Before turning to trends in relative quality measures, Tables 4.1 through 4.3 present summary statistics on characteristics of new hires and promotes into DoD labs, by grade and pay plan. The information in these tables provides a starting point for thinking about quality and provides the kinds of statistics that are usually used to assess quality in most studies. In the tables in this chapter, the emphasis is on the most important grades in each pay plan.

The general patterns are similar for the three pay plans at most levels. New hires naturally have substantially fewer prior years of service with the DoD; therefore, they have much less firm-specific human capital. For new hires to be as desirable as internal promotes for filling vacant job slots, the new hires must have a greater amount of general human capital and/or innate ability. Indeed, new hires do have more general human capital. They tend to be somewhat older, suggesting more labor market experience. They also tend to be more likely to have an M.A. or some other advanced degree.

Interestingly, new hires are less likely to earn the highest possible rating in their first year on the job. This is not surprising because they have more on-the-job training to undergo than do internal candidates. One would expect their performance to catch up or surpass incumbents over time as their greater general human capital, and perhaps greater innate ability, combine with their increasing firm-specific knowledge of their employer.

Table 4.1

Characteristics of New Hires and Promotes, GS Pay Plan

				Year Hired or Promoted				
				1982–84	1985–87	1988–90	1991–93	1994–96
			Grade 11					
New	N: 1982–84	847	M.A.	36%	29%	30%	47%	43%
hire	N: 1994–96	113	Ph.D., M.D., or law	13%	12%	5%	14%	9%
			Rating = 1	0%	0%	1%	2%	5%
			Age	35.5	34.7	33.9	31.7	33
			Years of service	3.6	2.7	2	1.9	2.1
			Grade 12					
New	N: 1982–84	1,329	M.A.	29%	27%	28%	24%	21%
hire	N: 1994–96	314	Ph.D., M.D., or law	32%	33%	32%	46%	54%
			Rating = 1	1%	1%	4%	6%	7%
			Age	39.1	38.9	36.4	35.1	36.3
			Years of service	4.8	3.7	3.2	2.3	2.5
Promote	N: 1982–84	1,914	M.A.	22%	16%	12%	12%	14%
	N: 1994–96	3,743	Ph.D., M.D., or law	5%	3%	1%	1%	1%
			Rating = 1	4%	3%	14%	19%	28%
			Age	33.6	31.8	30.4	30.4	30.4
			Years of service	7.8	6.6	5.9	5.7	6.3
			Grade 13					
New	N: 1982–84	119	M.A.	29%	30%	23%	24%	11%
hire	N: 1994–96	53	Ph.D., M.D., or law	51%	51%	52%	47%	83%
			Rating = 1	2%	1%	2%	9%	20%
			Age	43	42.5	41.7	41.6	39.3
			Years of service	5.6	6.7	4.5	3.6	2.2
Promote	N: 1982–84	867	M.A.	31%	30%	25%	24%	28%
	N: 1994–96	2,413	Ph.D., M.D., or law	11%	11%	10%	9%	11%
			Rating = 1	8%	13%	26%	35%	53%
			Age	39.5	39.7	38.1	36.3	36.1
			Years of service	13.6	13.5	11.6	10.4	10.9
			Grade 14					
New	N: 1982–84	55	M.A.	25%	9%	29%	14%	7%
hire	N: 1994–96	14	Ph.D., M.D., or law	58%	73%	58%	72%	93%
			Rating = 1	0%	0%	0%	0%	7%
			Age	48.5	48	45.5	44.8	43.1
			Years of service	10.1	6.5	4.8	4	1.8
Promote	N: 1982–84	199	M.A.	33%	32%	32%	29%	29%
	N: 1994–96	334	Ph.D., M.D., or law	28%	27%	20%	23%	22%
			Rating = 1	11%	16%	37%	44%	64%
			Age	43.3	43.5	43.6	42.5	42.1
			Years of service	17.5	18.1	17.7	15.9	16.5

Table 4.2

Characteristics of New Hires and Promotes, PMRS Pay Plan

				Year Hired or Promoted				
				1982–84	1985–87	1988–90	1991–93	1994–96
			Grade 13					
New	N: 1982–84	46	M.A.	31%	18%	29%	14%	25%
hire	N: 1994–96	4	Ph.D., M.D., or law	51%	63%	44%	73%	75%
			Rating = 1	0%	2%	4%	6%	0%
			Age	42.6	40.3	40.5	40.4	38.8
			Years of service	7	4.9	4.6	2.6	1
			Grade 14					
New	N: 1982–84	36	M.A.	27%	19%	26%	24%	25%
hire	N: 1994–96	4	Ph.D., M.D., or law	58%	73%	64%	66%	75%
			Rating = 1	3%	0%	7%	10%	0%
			Age	43.1	43.2	45.3	43.2	42.5
			Years of service	8.8	5.1	4.7	2.4	1.8
Promote	N: 1982–84	284	M.A.	34%	34%	31%	31%	28%
	N: 1994–96	95	Ph.D., M.D., or law	16%	18%	14%	17%	31%
			Rating = 1	5%	11%	20%	24%	52%
			Age	42.8	43.6	43.4	43.5	40.8
			Years of service	18.9	19.3	19.1	18.9	15.1
			Grade 15					
New	N: 1982–84	21	M.A.	42%	17%	21%	19%	33%
hire	N: 1994–96	3	Ph.D., M.D., or law	53%	75%	57%	75%	67%
			Rating = 1	5%	0%	17%	7%	33%
			Age	48.9	48.6	53	51.3	47.3
			Years of service	11.9	8.4	9.2	4.3	3
Promote	N: 1982–84	157	M.A.	40%	41%	38%	37%	44%
	N: 1994–96	114	Ph.D., M.D., or law	17%	26%	24%	23%	19%
			Rating = 1	12%	15%	28%	41%	55%
			Age	46.2	45.8	46.9	47.3	48
			Years of service	22.1	21	22.7	23	23

Table 4.4 presents comparisons of the performance of new hires to the performance of otherwise similar promotes. For each pay plan, regressions were run for groups of employees hired or promoted into a specific level at a specific interval. The regressions are intended to predict future performance, measured as the employee's salary growth, and predict whether the employee's most recent performance rating was 1 (the latter prediction employs linear probability models). Dummy variables for specific fiscal years and controls similar to those used for the regressions presented in Chapter Three, plus

Table 4.3

Characteristics of New Hires and Promotes, China Lake Pay Plan

				Year Hired or Promoted				
				1982–84	1985–87	1988–90	1991–93	1994–96
			Grade 1					
New	N: 1982–84	181	M.A.	8%	6%	4%	1%	9%
hire	N: 1994–96	68	Ph.D., M.D., or law	0%	0%	0%	0%	0%
			Rating = 1	—	0%	1%	0%	0%
			Age	25.7	26	26.4	26.1	28.6
			Years of service	1.7	1.7	1.6	1.6	2.7
			Grade 2					
New	N: 1982–84	61	M.A.	53%	32%	54%	55%	26%
hire	N: 1994–96	23	Ph.D., M.D., or law	29%	22%	17%	29%	35%
			Rating = 1	—	0%	0%	0%	0%
			Age	30	30.6	30.7	30.2	33.8
			Years of service	2.4	3.1	1.7	1.8	3.5
Promote	N: 1982–84	40	M.A.	—	7%	5%	3%	1%
	N: 1994–96	79	Ph.D., M.D., or law	—	0%	0%	0%	0%
			Rating = 1	—	0%	2%	7%	5%
			Age	29.8	27.8	28.2	28.6	28.9
			Years of service	4.3	4	3.7	4	5.3
			Grade 3					
New	N: 1982–84	55	M.A.	41%	33%	29%	31%	25%
hire	N: 1994–96	57	Ph.D., M.D., or law	21%	24%	26%	19%	10%
			Rating = 1	0%	0%	2%	20%	100%
			Age	41.6	42.9	41.2	43.4	40.2
			Years of service	6.4	4.6	3.2	6.8	3.2
Promote	N: 1982–84	28	M.A.	—	26%	21%	15%	16%
	N: 1994–96	386	Ph.D., M.D., or law	—	10%	8%	5%	4%
			Rating = 1	—	—	3%	6%	8%
			Age	35.3	33.6	32.4	32.1	31.9
			Years of service	7.6	8	7	6.7	6.7

education, are also included. All regressions in this chapter include controls for education, race, gender, veteran status, and region.

Salary growth is the percentage annualized change from the year the employee entered a particular grade until the current year.[2] Because new hires are often brought into salary grades at lower salary steps than promotes are, new hires might exhibit more rapid salary growth

---

[2]The mean is approximately 0.07 (7 percent per year).

Table 4.4

Performance of New Hires Versus Promotes

Year of Regression	N	GS Pay Plan			
		Wage Growth Regressions		Rating Linear Probability Models	
		New Hire	New Hire x Cohort	New Hire	New Hire x Cohort
Hired or Promoted into Grade 11					
1987	4,197	0.0641**	−0.0190*	−0.0308**	0.0162***
1990	8,411	0.0095***	−0.0031***	−0.0265	0.0053
1993	12,278	0.0193***	−0.0048***	0.0270	−0.0048
1996	13,446	0.0126***	−0.0020***	0.0239	−0.0047
Hired or Promoted into Grade 12					
1987	4,314	−0.0117***	0.0050***	−0.0495***	0.0219***
1990	8,479	0.0001	0.0005*	0.0063	−0.0011
1993	14,036	0.0152***	−0.0027***	0.0457**	−0.0046
1996	17,253	0.0055***	−0.0005***	0.0598**	−0.0040
Hired or Promoted into Grade 13					
1987	1,621	−0.0133**	0.0079***	−0.2284**	0.0754**
1990	2,917	−0.0053*	0.0021***	−0.1095	0.0207
1993	4,632	0.0100***	−0.0018***	0.0505	−0.0104
1996	6,082	0.0008	0.0004	0.0045	−0.0022
Hired or Promoted into Grade 14					
1987	320	−0.0216*	0.0115***	−0.0837	−0.0113
1990	703	0.0009	−0.0004	−0.2368*	0.0420
1993	1,176	0.0170***	−0.0039***	−0.0201	−0.0212
1996	1,328	−0.0001	0.0002	0.1891	−0.0198

Year of Regression	N	PMRS Pay Plan			
		Wage Growth Regressions		Rating Linear Probability Models	
		New Hire	New Hire x Cohort	New Hire	New Hire x Cohort
Hired or Promoted into Grade 13					
1987	71	−0.0430**	0.0132***	−0.3259	0.0333
1990	140	−0.0293**	0.0019	−0.0514	0.0475**
1993	211	0.0000	−0.0013***	0.2248	0.0277**
1996	178	−0.0057	0.0002	0.1812	0.0025
Hired or Promoted into Grade 14					
1987	886	−0.0376***	0.0133***	−0.3945***	0.1496***
1990	1,829	−0.0181***	0.0022**	−0.2422**	0.0692***
1993	2,572	−0.0001	−0.0020***	−0.1415	0.0118
1996	1,991	−0.0119***	0.0004	−0.0621	0.0045

Table 4.4 (continued)

| | | China Lake Pay Plan | | | |
| | | Wage Growth Regressions | | Rating Linear Probability Models | |
Year of Regression	N	New Hire	New Hire x Cohort	New Hire	New Hire x Cohort
		Hired or Promoted into Grade 2			
1990	99	0.0209*	–0.0032	0.1437	–0.0236
1993	143	0.0079	–0.0027	0.0195	–0.0224
1996	117	–0.0118	0.0003	0.0929	–0.0110
		Hired or Promoted into Grade 3			
1990	107	–0.0224***	0.0036**	–0.2421*	0.0398
1993	182	0.0078	–0.0019	–0.0656	–0.0135
1996	175	–0.0010	–0.0001	–0.2928*	0.0340**

NOTES: ***= significant at 1%; **= at 5%; *= at 10%.

over the first few years in a grade as they are brought into line with promotes. This would, in some sense, overstate relative salary growth of new hires because part of the growth would be due to administrative practices rather than individual performance. It might also downward bias any measured trend in relative performance of new hires because the effect would be strongest in the early years for new hires. To control for this, the employee's first step on entry into the grade was included in regressions for the GS and China Lake pay plans (the PMRS plan does not have steps).

Each regression includes a dummy variable for whether the employee was hired into a particular level instead of being promoted into it. The coefficient gives some indication of overall performance of new hires versus incumbents. Each regression also controls for the year the employee entered that grade (that is, the employee's cohort). Finally, the new-hire dummy was interacted with the cohort in order to search for trends in the quality of new hires compared with promotes. Table 4.4 shows regressions for every third year to get a view of any possible evolution in trends. The only coefficients shown are for the new-hire dummy and its interaction with the cohort.

There is little to suggest *a priori* that new-hire coefficients should be anything other than zero. New hires and promotes into the same grade should theoretically be relatively equal in their ability or human capital, otherwise the DoD would presumably prefer the more qualified group. Given that less is known about new hires initially, they present a greater risk for the DoD than promotes. To the extent that the DoD is risk averse or there are turnover costs, the DoD may require a higher expected performance level from a new hire for it to prefer the new hire over an internal candidate.

Indeed, Table 4.4 indicates that new hires did perform a little better than internal candidates overall. Most new hire coefficients are positive, especially for later regressions that cover more of the sample period. In particular, new hires seem to achieve faster annual wage growth, even after controlling for the salary step at which they started (for the GS and China Lake pay plans). However, these effects are often statistically or economically insignificant.

Of greater interest are the interaction terms. These are almost always very small in size. For example, the annual wage growth for a new hire into GS Grade 11 has a downward trend of about 0.2 percent per cohort more than the annual wage growth for promotes for the full sample. The strongest evidence from the salary growth regressions of a deterioration in the quality of new hires is for Grade 11, in which all trends are negative and statistically significant in this case. In the other grades or pay plans, trends seen in the salary growth regression are either statistically insignificant or sometimes positive and sometimes negative. In short, there is no systematically derived evidence, from the salary growth regressions, of any important decline in the relative quality of new hires.

The performance rating regressions show even less evidence of any trend in the relative quality of new hires. Almost all of the interaction terms are statistically indistinguishable from zero (despite the often large sample sizes).[3]

The analyses in this chapter provide little basis for arguing that the DoD experienced a decline in its ability to recruit quality scientists and engineers into its labs over the 1982 through 1996 period, at least relative to the quality of internal candidates for promotion. This is

---

[3]More informally, the evidence in Chapter Three suggests that returns to skills declined in the GS pay plan, possibly declined a little in the China Lake pay plans, and had little change in the PMRS pay plan. Therefore, it is interesting to note that if Table 4.4 shows any evidence of a decline in the quality of new hires, it would be in the GS pay plan at Grade 11 and possibly Grade 12. This rough pattern is consistent with the evidence given in Chapter Three, although it is admittedly a very weak pattern.

true for the GS, PMRS, and China Lake pay plans. This report now turns to the final empirical analysis in the study, which compares those employees who exit to those who stay with the DoD.

Chapter Five

RETENTION OF HIGH-QUALITY SCIENTISTS AND ENGINEERS

This chapter presents analyses of the DoD's ability to retain quality scientists and engineers. In this case, instead of following employees forward from the point at which they enter a given grade, as was done in Chapter Four, *previous* performance is compared between those lab employees who stay and those who exit from the DoD for a given grade in a given year. Before turning to those analyses, Tables 5.1 through 5.3 present summary statistics on characteristics of exits and stays for each pay plan.

The big question addressed in this chapter is whether the DoD had difficulty retaining high-quality S/Es who might otherwise have stayed if the DoD's compensation more closely tracked pay in the private sector. Therefore, we are interested in separations here, not retirements. In addition, the DoD offered early retirement incentives during the drawdown of the 1990s. The data in this study distinguish between separations and retirements. To further avoid the possibility of coding an early retirement as a separation, analyses in this chapter consider only those employees younger than 54. Separation and retirement rates jump dramatically at age 54 because many employees entering the fiscal year at age 54 will become eligible for various retirement options when they turn 55 during the year. The data in this report are from the beginning of fiscal years.

It is not clear *a priori* whether those who stay should have better or worse quality or performance measures than those who exit. Employees leave for several reasons, including how well they expect to perform in alternative employment relative to their current jobs. In a

Table 5.1

Characteristics of Exits and Stays, GS Pay Plan

				Year Exiting or Staying				
				1982–84	1985–87	1988–90	1991–93	1994–96
			Grade 11					
Exit	N (1982–84)	392	M.A.	33%	24%	16%	28%	21%
	N (1994–96)	422	Ph.D., M.D., or law	5%	5%	3%	2%	2%
			Rating = 1	2%	2%	9%	15%	18%
			Age	30.8	29.2	29.2	30.2	30.9
			Years of service	5.6	4.5	4.5	4.9	6.8
Stay	N (1982–84)	8,882	MA	27%	18%	14%	15%	17%
	N (1994–96)	6,656	Ph.D., M.D., or law	4%	3%	1%	1%	1%
			Rating = 1	3%	2%	10%	14%	22%
			Age	33.4	31.3	30.3	30.6	32.3
			Years of service	8.1	6.4	5.6	5.7	7.4
			Grade 12					
Exit	N (1982–84)	778	M.A.	51%	42%	32%	30%	31%
	N (1994–96)	1,500	Ph.D., M.D., or law	27%	26%	20%	10%	7%
			Rating = 1	8%	6%	17%	19%	27%
			Age	35.7	34.9	33.4	33.7	34.2
			Years of service	9.8	8.7	7.9	8.9	10.0
Stay	N (1982–84)	30,044	M.Al	35%	34%	26%	21%	26%
	N (1994–96)	43,861	Ph.D., M.D., or law	10%	11%	8%	5%	4%
			Rating = 1	7%	6%	15%	21%	31%
			Age	38.6	38.1	36.1	35	35.6
			Years of service	13.8	12.9	11.1	10.2	10.9
			Grade 13					
Exit	N (1982–84)	200	M.A.	108%	81%	51%	52%	64%
	N (1994–96)	299	Ph.D., M.D., or law	64%	62%	42%	31%	33%
			Rating = 1	12%	19%	19%	30%	49%
			Age	41.6	39.3	41.3	39.5	39.7
			Years of service	14.7	12.9	15.1	13.5	14.9
Stay	N (1982–84)	12,831	M.A.	57%	60%	57%	53%	62%
	N (1994–96)	15,648	Ph.D., M.D., or law	21%	20%	20%	18%	19%
			Rating = 1	9%	18%	24%	34%	53%
			Age	43	42.8	41.6	40.4	40.1
			Years of service	18.7	18.1	16.5	15.2	15.1
			Grade 14					
Exit	N (1982–84)	57	M.A.	15%	30%	28%	26%	16%
	N (1994–96)	62	Ph.D., M.D., or law	51%	47%	35%	42%	39%
			Rating = 1	0%	36%	19%	25%	53%
			Age	43.5	42.2	45.3	45.1	44.9
			Years of service	17	15.8	20.3	16.6	19.8

Table 5.1 (continued)

				Year Exiting or Staying				
				1982–84	1985–87	1988–90	1991–93	1994–96
Stay	N (1982–84)	4,480	M.A.	34%	33%	34%	35%	38%
	N (1994–96)	4,092	Ph.D.	26%	31%	27%	25%	24%
			Rating = 1	12%	24%	34%	43%	64%
			Age	44.9	45.3	44.8	44.1	44.4
			Years of service	20.1	20.2	19.5	18.7	19.2
			Grade 15					
Exit	N (1982–84)	21	M.A.	10%	33%	17%	11%	19%
	N (1994–96)	16	Ph.D.	65%	67%	83%	89%	69%
			Rating = 1	0%	10%	0%	44%	50%
			Age	46.2	45.6	52	47.6	48.3
			Years of service	18.3	12.1	21.2	20.9	21.2
Stay	N (1982–84)	1,275	M.A.	30%	23%	20%	23%	34%
	N (1994–96)	736	Ph.D.	34%	55%	63%	60%	44%
			Rating = 1	8%	28%	38%	42%	71%
			Age	46.3	47	46.9	47.6	47.4
			Years of service	21.3	20.5	20.6	21.4	21.6

simple labor economics model, higher performers would be more likely to stay because high performance indicates a good job match or high firm-specific human capital. But the more bureaucratic nature of the DoD's personnel systems compared with the private sector may cause higher-performing employees to be more likely to leave and low performers to be more likely to stay.

Indeed, few clear patterns in the characteristics of stays versus exits emerge from any of the pay plans. Those who exit tend to have slightly more general human capital in the form of education but slightly less firm-specific human capital in years of service. They are also generally slightly younger. Performance ratings of those who stay tend to be a little better than those who leave. Regardless of interpretations, what is of interest in this study is the *trends* in the measures for those who stay relative to those who leave. These are examined in Table 5.4.

Table 5.4 presents results from linear probability models predicting whether or not an employee will exit from the DoD, as a function of measures of the employee's skill and performance (plus year dummies and the usual controls). The measures of skill are dummies for an M.A. or Ph.D. The measures of performance are the employee's annualized percentage salary growth from the time the employee

Table 5.2

Characteristics of Exits and Stays, PMRS Pay Plan

				Year Exiting or Staying				
				1982–84	1985–87	1988–90	1991–93	1994–96
			Grade 13					
Exit	N (1982–84)	125	M.A.	34%	29%	22%	24%	34%
	N (1994–96)	263	Ph.D., M.D., or law	16%	24%	22%	15%	8%
			Rating = 1	3%	9%	19%	24%	27%
			Age	40.7	39.2	38.3	38.4	43
			Years of service	15.8	13.9	12.8	13.8	19.6
Stay	N (1982–84)	5,906	M.A.	31%	30%	28%	26%	29%
	N (1994–96)	8,862	Ph.D., M.D., or law	8%	12%	12%	10%	11%
			Rating = 1	4%	7%	16%	21%	37%
			Age	42.8	42.5	41.8	41	41.8
			Years of service	19	18.6	17.7	17	17.9
			Grade 14					
Exit	N (1982–84)	67	M.A.	40%	23%	31%	29%	37%
	N (1994–96)	151	Ph.D., M.D., or law	35%	40%	32%	29%	18%
			Rating = 1	16%	13%	19%	31%	37%
			Age	43	42.7	44.9	45.7	47.5
			Years of service	17.5	17.2	19.3	20.9	25.3
Stay	N (1982–84)	4,659	M.A.	39%	39%	38%	39%	41%
	N (1994–96)	7,160	Ph.D.	16%	18%	16%	15%	16%
			Rating = 1	9%	13%	23%	32%	52%
			Age	44.5	44.8	44.9	45	45.8
			Years of service	20.5	21	21.1	21.2	21.9
			Grade 15					
Exit	N (1982–84)	27	M.A.	20%	31%	32%	20%	45%
	N (1994–96)	76	Ph.D.	40%	55%	36%	53%	27%
			Rating = 1	23%	29%	38%	45%	65%
			Age	44.9	44.8	47.9	48.2	50.4
			Years of service	15.5	17.6	23.6	22.5	27.7
Stay	N (1982–84)	2,107	M.A.	36%	36%	38%	40%	44%
	N (1994–96)	3,349	Ph.D.	25%	29%	30%	29%	30%
			Rating = 1	16%	23%	38%	52%	73%
			Age	46.4	46.7	47.1	47.5	48.2
			Years of service	21.9	22.4	23.1	23.6	24.3

entered the DoD until the present year and a dummy for whether the most recent performance rating was equal to 1 (the highest performance rating). All of these measures are made to interact with years in order to search for trends in their effect on DoD retention or exit from the DoD. The table shows only the coefficients for the four skill and performance measures and their interaction terms.

Table 5.3

Characteristics of Exits and Stays, China Lake Pay Plan

| | | | | Year Exiting or Staying | | | | |
				1982–84	1985–87	1988–90	1991–93	1994–96
			Grade 1					
Exit	N (1982–84)	23	M.A.	0%	0%	0%	0%	0%
			Ph.D., M.D., or law	0%	0%	0%	0%	0%
	N (1994–96)	11	Rating = 1	—	0%	0%	0%	0%
			Age	26.2	26.3	26.4	26.1	28.7
			Years of service	3	2.1	1.7	2	5.5
Stay	N (1982–84)	282	M.A.	0%	0%	0%	0%	0%
			Ph.D., M.D., or law	0%	0%	0%	0%	0%
	N (1994–96)	160	Rating = 1	—	0%	2%	2%	0%
			Age	26.4	26.5	27.2	27.4	28.5
			Years of service	2.3	2.3	2.6	2.8	4.1
			Grade 2					
Exit	N (1982–84)	21	M.A.	0%	14%	4%	11%	2%
			Ph.D., M.D., or law	0%	14%	4%	11%	2%
	N (1994–96)	52	Rating = 1	—	0%	0%	0%	0%
			Age	28.7	30.9	30.6	31.3	32.6
			Years of service	4.6	4.5	4.8	5	7.7
Stay	N (1982–84)	382	M.A.	13%	10%	4%	4%	2%
			Ph.D., M.D., or law	13%	10%	4%	4%	2%
	N (1994–96)	914	Rating = 1	0%	0%	3%	7%	5%
			Age	32.2	30.7	30.4	30.7	32
			Years of service	6.3	5.4	5.1	5.1	6.7
			Grade 3					
Exit	N (1982–84)	37	M.A.	9%	20%	18%	9%	3%
			Ph.D., M.D., or law	9%	20%	18%	9%	3%
	N (1994–96)	254	Rating = 1	0%	33%	6%	13%	2%
			Age	40.5	39.8	36.7	39.2	38.6
			Years of service	13.4	11.7	10.1	14.7	14.4
Stay	N (1982–84)	2,310	MA	12%	12%	11%	10%	5%
			Ph.D., M.D., or law	12%	12%	11%	10%	5%
	N (1994–96)	9,338	Rating = 1	0%	4%	4%	6%	5%
			Age	41.8	42.2	41.4	40.4	39.4
			Years of service	16.7	16.7	15.7	14.8	14.6
			Grade 4					
Stay	N (1982–84)	541	M.A.	26%	23%	21%	21%	15%
			Ph.D., M.D., or law	26%	23%	21%	21%	15%
	N (1994–96)	1,396	Rating = 1	0%	11%	9%	12%	19%
			Age	46.3	46.6	46.8	47.1	47.7
			Years of service	22.2	22.6	22.9	23.1	24.3

Table 5.4

Retention of High-Quality S/Es

	GS Pay Plan				
	Grade 11	Grade 12	Grade 13	Grade 14	Grade 15
Salary growth	0.3809	−11.3406***	−18.7958***	13.9805	−51.1636*
Salary growth x year	−0.0002	0.0057***	0.0095***	−0.0070	0.0257*
Rating = 1	−3.2438	−0.0814	0.9473	2.0024	−1.8610
(Rating = 1) x year	0.0016	0.0000	−0.0005	−0.0010	0.0009
M.A.	−0.8444	0.9136**	0.9210**	0.1540	1.1349
M.A. x year	0.0004	−0.0005**	−0.0005**	−0.0001	−0.0006
PhD	−7.4335	3.4435***	1.1515*	1.1945	0.2383
Ph.D. x year	0.0038	−0.0017***	−0.0006*	−0.0006	−0.0001
N	49,008	178,829	67,241	17,647	2,676

	PMRS Pay Plan		
	Grade 13	Grade 14	Grade 15
Salary growth	7.4148	−22.0674***	−1.6888
Salary growth x year	−0.0037	0.0111**	0.0009
Rating = 1	3.4691**	1.1680	1.0966
(Rating = 1) x year	−0.0017**	−0.0006	−0.0005
M.A.	−0.9189	−0.1084	−0.0518
M.A.x year	0.0005	0.0001	0.0000
Ph.D.	3.3746***	2.8228***	2.0621***
Ph.D. x year	−0.0017***	−0.0014***	−0.0010***
N	42,616	43,872	24,201

	China Lake Pay Plan		
	Grade 2	Grade 3	Grade 4
Salary growth	33.8822	3.2549	−41.9922
Salary growth x year	−0.0170	−0.0016	0.0211
Rating = 1	9.3007	7.9809**	7.2429**
(Rating = 1) x year	−0.0047	−0.0040**	−0.0036**
M.A.	−8.6546	1.6848	1.4105
M.A. x year	0.0044	−0.0008	−0.0007
Ph.D.	−6.9591	5.8609***	−0.5445
Ph.D. x year	0.0035	−0.0029***	0.0003
N	2,548	20,122	5,584

NOTES: ***= significant at 1%; **= at 5%, *= at 10%. Regressions include controls for race, gender, veteran status, and region.

The results reported in Table 5.4 reveal some tendency for Ph.D.'s to be more likely to leave the DoD, and a similar tendency for M.A.'s in the GS pay plan. S/Es who earn better performance ratings also have a somewhat higher tendency to leave, although this is a weaker result. Generally, though, few coefficients are statistically significant. Therefore, retention does not seem to be systematically weaker or stronger for high-quality or high-performance lab S/Es. As discussed earlier in this chapter, this is not necessarily surprising; high-quality S/Es may have good outside alternatives but they may also have good job matches within the DoD.

The interaction terms for each of the quality or performance indicators show almost no evidence of trends over time. Almost none of the interaction terms are statistically significant, and all are very small in economic significance. Because these regressions predict exits, a trend toward lower quality of retained employees would be indicated by positive signs on the interaction terms in Table 5.4. In fact, the interaction terms have no clear pattern in this regard. Therefore, the suggestion in this chapter of any decline in the quality of DoD S/E lab employees over the sample period is even weaker than what Chapter Four suggests.

Chapter Six

CONCLUSIONS

This report presents an analysis of pay competitiveness and quality of civil-service scientific and engineering personnel in DoD laboratories. These personnel are of increasing importance to the DoD given the changes in its mission, the rapid pace of technological advancement, and the DoD's growing use of high technology in weapons and systems design.

Federal pay systems are centralized, simple, and rigid in structure. These pay system characteristics have many benefits, including simplified personnel management and perceived equity across divisions. However, these characteristics can also make it difficult for managers to respond effectively to changes in the private-sector labor market that may affect their ability to adequately staff their work groups.

Moreover, federal pay systems have not evolved over time. In contrast, compensation structures changed dramatically in the private sector over the 1980s and 1990s due in large part to skill-based technological change that drove up returns to skills. These changes should, presumably, place increasing pressure on the competitiveness of pay for the DoD S/E workforce over time.

How the competitiveness of pay affects the quality of the S/E segment of the DoD workforce has long been an issue of concern, but there has been little quantitative evidence to assess whether this is a potential problem for the DoD. This report provides just such a quantitative analysis of this issue.

One key feature of this study is the analysis of DMDC personnel data, which allow for a micro view of compensation. The data also allow for longitudinal analyses of individual careers.

Finally, this report emphasizes *trends* in the relative quality of DoD S/E personnel. This approach is particularly informative about changes in the DoD's ability to attract and retain talented scientists and engineers.

This study found that despite changes in private-sector wage structures entailing an increase in returns to observed and unobserved skills over the 1980s and 1990s, returns to skills did not rise significantly among scientific and engineering personnel in DoD laboratories over this period. If anything, some evidence exists that returns to skills declined for employees in the most important pay plan, GS, although they may have risen slightly for employees in the PMRS pay plan. While this is in stark contrast to what has been observed in the private sector, it is not surprising given the unchanging and centralized pay and personnel systems in the DoD. This evidence is also consistent with the findings of Katz and Krueger (1991) for the federal government as a whole, and is consistent with their conclusion that rigid federal pay systems make it difficult for the federal sector to adapt its compensation systems to changes in the private-sector labor market.

A second major finding is that despite a lack of increasing returns to skills for lab S/Es, little evidence exists that the DoD suffered a decline in its ability to attract and retain high-quality laboratory personnel from 1982 through 1996. There were no clear or significant trends in the quality or performance of new hires relative to incumbents, or employees the DoD retained relative to those who left the DoD.

This report focuses on trends in the relative quality of those employees entering and leaving the DoD laboratory workforce. Therefore, the report does not address the overall *level* of quality of these employees. Indeed, it was argued that such an assessment is inherently subjective, at least given the data used here. Therefore, it is possible that the DoD does have difficulty in recruiting and retaining quality scientists and engineers for its laboratories.

Nevertheless, what this report can conclude with some certainty is that the data studied here show little convincing evidence that the magnitude of the problem worsened (or improved) from 1982 through 1996. This in itself is a somewhat surprising finding, given the rhetoric of various reports and commissions that have examined similar issues, and given the changes observed in the private sector over this period.

These results are not necessarily inconsistent with the DoD's inability to keep pace with changes in private-sector compensation systems over this period. One reason that the DoD appears to have experienced little decline in its ability to attract and retain a quality S/E workforce, despite falling behind in returns to skills compared with the overall private sector, is suggested by the work of Rosen and Ryoo (1997), who studied the private-sector labor market for engineers in the United States. They found that the labor market exhibits relatively high elasticities of supply and demand for engineers and therefore adjusts relatively rapidly to changes in supply or demand.

Private-sector defense work tends to be quite different from work done for other industries in the private sector and is actually more similar to work done within the DoD. Indeed, many scientists and engineers in the defense sector switch their employment between the DoD and defense contractors with regularity. This suggests that there may be an important element of *defense-industry-specific* human capital in this sector for scientists and engineers.

Given that the private defense sector was hit hard by downsizing during the same period as the DoD drawdown, and given the sector's relatively quick adjustments to at least the engineering labor market, it may be that private-sector opportunities for DoD S/Es did *not* increase much during the sample period in comparison with other sectors of the private labor market. For example, there was a flood of unemployed scientists and engineers in the defense sector in Southern California during the 1980s (Schoeni et al., 1996). An engineer working for the DoD at that time might not have had attractive employment alternatives outside the DoD. If so, it would not be surprising that even though DoD compensation systems failed to adapt to changes in the economy as much as private-sector pay systems had done during the 1980s and 1990s, the DoD did not experience a decline in its ability to recruit and retain high-quality scientists and engineers. Although this explanation is plausible, further analysis of it is beyond the scope of this study.

There are other possible interpretations of the evidence presented here. It may be that S/E quality did decline over the sample period but the methods employed in this study are inadequate to measure this decline. The quality measures employed here involve comparison of job and wage mobility across cohorts. Although pay growth should be an indicator of quality, it is an imperfect measure, especially when the DoD pay systems are relatively rigid and inflexible in the first place.

Another possible explanation is that DoD pay levels were *above* market levels at the beginning of the sample period, but became aligned with the external labor market over time (that is, the external market caught up). If so, the quality of S/Es might not decline substantially, even if pay declines, if S/Es were earning *rents* (higher than competitive compensation levels) from employment at the DoD in the early years of the study.

Or, it may be that DoD S/Es were not of relatively high quality prior to 1985; a hypothesis maintained in this report is that pay levels *do* affect the quality of DoD scientists and engineers. It is possible, although it seems unlikely and is impossible to test with these data, that DoD recruitment and retention mechanisms are themselves so rigid that compensation levels do not materially affect the quality of S/Es.

Another point for the DoD to consider is how the response to changes in external opportunities might vary across S/Es of differing quality. Figures 2.1 and 2.2 earlier in this report suggest that DoD compensation levels are no higher, and are likely somewhat lower, than those for comparable private-sector S/Es. Given the relative inflexibility of DoD pay systems, this should apply even more to high-quality DoD S/Es.

Therefore, high-quality DoD S/Es have chosen to remain with the DoD presumably because of factors other than compensation, such as a strong personal match with the DoD's work environment or interesting project assignments. As such, high-quality S/Es in DoD labs are likely to have less-elastic responses to private-sector compensation. But, even if this is the case, the findings of this study are still of potential concern to the DoD.

After the private defense sector completely adjusts to the post–cold-war era, the DoD might find that its compensation practices are out of date compared with the private sector. This might lead to future problems in managing the quality of the S/E workforce. Furthermore, the demographics of the S/E workforce changed because of the way in which the DoD implemented the drawdown. It created an older S/E workforce, with bulging numbers in the middle grades and mid-career ages, and few new hires in recent years. This demographic shift may create an S/E workforce that is not up-to-date on the latest technological advances. It may also mean that the DoD will have difficulty in attracting quality S/Es in the future, if and when it increases its hiring rates, because of clogged job promotion ladders.

One interesting finding is that at least for scientists and engineers in the DoD laboratories, the PMRS and China Lake pay systems did *not* markedly improve the DoD's ability to develop a quality S/E workforce. Apparently, the stronger performance incentives intended with the PMRS plan were not that much stronger in practice, nor did they improve the DoD's ability to recruit and retain technical employees.

The findings are also in contrast to the generally favorable analyses of the China Lake plan (see Chapter Two). The China Lake plan is a "broadband" plan (that is, it has fewer salary grades, but the grades have substantially broader ranges between minimum and maximum salary). While salary grades are not as broad in the GS plan, similar promotion possibilities exist for most S/Es studied here because the GS plan has a comparable number of effective salary grades (11 through 15) for its S/E workforce. Therefore, while salary growth may be smaller under the GS plan, S/Es may end up with similar ultimate salary levels.

A recurrent theme of this study is that pay comparability is not simply a question of the level of pay—it is also about the *structure* of pay, which involves a set of pay levels and promotion paths over an employee's career. Pay systems involve rewarding skills, human capital, and other dimensions of quality and performance, as well as relative levels of compensation across various levels of responsibility. There is no reason to believe that the complex system linking pay to these various dimensions should be static over time. However, the design of federal pay systems makes them extremely rigid, whereas compensation systems in the private sector exhibit a great deal of evolution. It is the federal pay system's inherent inflexibility and inability to adapt to labor market forces that may be the most important issues in the design of future DoD compensation systems.

Asch, Beth J., and John T. Warner, *Separation and Retirement Incentives in the Civil Service: A Comparison of FERS and CSRS*, Santa Monica, Calif.: RAND, MR-986-OSD, 1999.

_____, *A Theory of Military Compensation and Personnel Policy*, Santa Monica, Calif.: RAND, MR-439-OSD, 1994.

Bound, John, and George J. Johnson, "Changes in the Structure of Wages During the 1980s: An Evaluation of Alternative Explanations," *American Economic Review*, Vol. 82, No. 3, 1992, pp. 371–392.

Campbell, Alan K., and Linda S. Dix, eds., *Recruitment, Retention, and Utilization of Federal Scientists and Engineers: A Report to the Carnegie Commission on Science, Technology, and Government*, Washington, D.C.: National Academy Press, 1990.

Campbell, Alan K., Stephen J. Lukasik, and Michael G. H. McGeary, eds., *Improving the Recruitment, Retention, and Utilization of Federal Scientists and Engineers: A Report to the Carnegie Commission on Science, Technology, and Government*, Washington D.C.: National Academy Press, 1993.

Doeringer, Peter, and Michael Piore, *Internal Labor Markets and Manpower Analysis*, Lexington, Mass.: M.E. Sharpe, 1985.

Ferrall, Christopher, "Levels of Responsibility in Jobs and the Distribution of Earnings Among U.S. Engineers, 1961–1986," *Industrial and Labor Relations Review*, Vol. 49, No. 1, 1995, pp. 150–169.

Gottschalk, Peter, and Sheldon Danzinger, eds., *Uneven Tides: Rising Inequality in America,* New York: Russell Sage Foundation, 1993.

Juhn, Chinhui, Kevin M. Murphy, and Brooks Pierce, "Wage Inequality and the Rise in the Returns to Skill," *Journal of Political Economy,* Vol. 101, No. 3, 1993, pp. 410–422.

Katz, Lawrence F., and Alan B. Krueger, "Changes in the Structure of Wages in the Public and Private Sectors," *Research in Labor Economics,* Vol. 12, 1991, pp. 137–172.

Katz, Lawrence F., and Kevin M. Murphy, "Changes in Relative Wages, 1963–1987: Supply and Demand Factors," *Quarterly Journal of Economics,* Vol. 107, No. 1, 1992, pp. 35–78.

Lazear, Edward P., *Personnel Economics for Managers,* New York: John Wiley & Sons, 1998.

Levy, Frank, and Richard J. Murname, "U.S. Earnings Levels and Earnings Inequality: A Review of Recent Trends and Proposed Explanations," *Journal of Economic Literature,* Vol. 30, No. 3, 1992, pp. 1333–1381.

Mace, Don, and Eric Yoder, eds., *Federal Employees Almanac 1995,* Reston, Va.: Federal Employees News Digest, Inc., 1995.

Main, Brian, Charles O'Reilly, and James Wade, "Top Executive Pay: Tournament or Teamwork," *Journal of Labor Economics,* Vol. 11, No. 4, 1993, pp. 607–628.

Mishel, Lawrence, Jared Bernstein, and John Schmitt, *The State of Working America,* Washington, D.C.: Economic Policy Institute, 1997.

Moulton, Brent, "A Reexamination of the Federal-Private Wage Differential in the United States," *Journal of Labor Economics,* Vol. 8, No. 2, 1990, pp. 270–293.

Murphy, Kevin M., and Finis Welch, "The Structure of Wages," *Quarterly Journal of Economics,* Vol. 107, No. 1. 1992, pp. 285–325.

National Science Foundation, *Characteristics of Recent Science and Engineering Graduates,* Arlington, Va., 1982, 1996, and 1993.

O'Shaughnessy, K. C., David I. Levine, and Peter Cappelli, "Changes in Managerial Pay Structures 1986–1992 and Rising Returns to Skill," Institute of Industrial Relations Working Paper No. 67, University of California at Berkeley, 1998.

Rosen, Sherwin, and Jaewoo Ryoo, "The Engineering Labor Market," working paper, The University of Chicago, 1997.

Schoeni, Robert F., Michael Dardia, Kevin F. McCarthy, and Georges Vernez, *Life After Cutbacks: Tracking California's Aerospace Workers,* Santa Monica, Calif.: RAND, MR-688-OSD, 1996.

U.S. Congressional Budget Office, "Comparing Federal Salaries with Those in the Private Sector," CBO memorandum, Washington, D.C., 1997.

U.S. Department of Labor, *Professional, Administrative, Clerical and Technical Pay Survey,* Washington, D.C., various years.

U.S. Office of Personnel Management, *A Summary Assessment of the Navy Demonstration Project,* Management Report IX, Washington, D.C., 1986.